Poems of Kim Yideum, Kim Haengsook & Kim Min Jeong

Poems of Kim Yideum, Kim Haengsook & Kim Min Jeong
Asia Pacific Poetry Series 10

First published 2017 by Vagabond Press
PO Box 958 Newtown NSW 2042 Australia
www.vagabondpress.net

Kim Yideum, Kim Haengsook & Kim Min Jeong © 2016
English translations, **Don Mee Choi, Johannes Göransson,
Jiyoon Lee, Jake Levine** © 2016

Cover image: Fi Jae Lee © 2015.
내 몸의 전세계 (*The Whole World on My Body*).
Mixed Media. Courtesy of the artist.

Designed and typeset by Michael Brennan.

Poems of Kim Yideum, Kim Haengsook & Kim Min Jeong is published
with the support of the Literature Translation Institute of Korea (LTI Korea).

ISBN 978-1-922181-37-4

Poems of Kim Yideum, Kim Haengsook & Kim Min Jeong

Translated from Korean
by Don Mee Choi, Johannes Göransson,
Jiyoon Lee & Jake Levine

With an introduction by Jake Levine

Vagabond Press | Asia Pacific Poetry Series

CONTENTS

Kim Haeng Sook

WHAT IS FUTURE-WAVE?
IS FUTURE-WAVE EVEN
A THING?

The three poets in this collection, Kim Yi-deum, Kim Min Jeong and Kim Haengsook debuted in the early 2000's, a turning point in the history of Korean culture. It was at this time, in the shadow of the national debt crisis and IMF bailout, when the Korean Wave known as *hallyu* began to gain traction. If the 1988 hosting of the Olympics in Seoul acted as an invitation for South Korea to be considered an advanced "democratic" nation in the eyes of the international community, then we might consider the 2002 co-hosting of the World Cup to be the moment at which South Korea had arrived. President Kim Dae Jung's project to expand governmental spending on cultural exports accelerated the push of Korean cultural products in the global market. Korean cinema entered what would later be seen as the beginning of its golden age. A new crop of young directors such as Park Chan-wook, Hong Sang Su and Kim Ki

Duk began garnering international success with films like *Oldboy* and *Spring, Summer, Fall, Winter.* The sales of Korean cars and electronics accelerated abroad. Freshly approved for new lines of consumer credit, the Korean population began to consume a wide variety of international products imported into the country for the first time. From the ashes of an industrial economy, the cogs of the K-pop machine began to turn. Korean culture caught the attention of an international audience on the world stage, and the various businesses and government entities that support and own rights to that structure began to tighten their grip on the spectacular brand identity they would market and sell to the world. Of course this identity would come to be dominated by cellphones, cars, plastic surgery, choreographed dance routines, boy bands, and fermented foods, but also it would be accompanied by a high culture of homegrown literature, film, and art. It is during this tumultuous period when the poetic movement known as *Miraepa*, or Future-wave, took shape.

The coming out party of the new generation of poets received a mixed reception. Scholars negatively criticized the work as frivolous, exhaustive, and sloppy, complaining that the poetry lacked the direct social and political message of previous generations.[1] Whereas we can say the early modernists of the Japanese colonial period were occupied with solving the problem of creating a literary voice for the future of the nation (much in the way American intellectuals looked to Walt Whitman in the 19th century), and postwar

1. Hyŏg-ung Kwŏn. *Miraep'a: Saeroun Si Wa Siin Ŭl Wihayŏ: Kwŏn Hyŏg-ung Pip'yŏngjip.* (Sŏul: Munhak Kwa Chisŏngsa, 2005), 148.

modernity aimed to locate reality in the whirlwind of a democracy overthrown by a military coup and ensuing Park Chung Hee dictatorship, what did *Miraepa* want to solve? What was at stake?

> *From the third, fourth, seventh rung of the ladder between heaven and hell, I'll caress the cards that are dealt to me until I'm destitute.*
>
> Kim Haengsook, *"Hormonography"*

The Asian financial crisis and IMF bailout of 1997 halted a 30 year period of rapid growth for South Korea, when GDP per capita went from just over $100 dollars in 1962 to over $20,000 in 2006. The economy was completely restructured as a precondition to the IMF bailout. The long period of growth that was driven by government led-investment and protection would now be controlled by the forces of a "free" global market. In the political imagination of many people, liberal democracy came to be associated with a widening gap of social inequality, while memories of the oppressive authoritarian regime of Park Chung Hee became romanticized for a national growth that was unprecedented in world history. All of a sudden it was as if the nation had been shocked out of history, where narratives of struggle, narratives of democratic freedom were flipped on their head. Just as the American supported politics of political dictatorships could not be separated from the economy during an era of unprecedented growth, the arrival of liberal democracy went "hand in hand with a crippling depression in the Asian region."[2] Naomi Klein in her groundbreaking book *The Shock Doctrine* wrote that the IMF bailout equated the annulment of democracy. South Koreans were told they could vote, but that their vote would have no bearing on the managing and organization of their economy. Hence the day that the deal was signed became known in Korea as "National Humiliation Day."[3]

> *But on a quiet day like today*
> *I hear the sound of the dead breathing*
> *from everywhere, anywhere. How is it possible?*
>
> *I need to speak now or never,*
> *for the intensity of guilt is slowly fading.*

Kim Yi-deum, "There is a Word Ghost"

The IMF crisis did not pass, it became the chaos-state of everyday life. Middle-class households shrunk from 75 percent in 1995 to 67 percent in 2010, while college educated heads of households doubled from 20 to over 40 percent.[4] Meanwhile household debt swelled from 187

2. Bruce Cummings. "The Asian Crisis, Democracy, and the End of Late Development"," in *The Politics of the Asian Economic Crisis,* edited by T.J Pempel, (Ithaca: Cornell University Press, 1999), 19.

3. Naomi Klein. *The Shock Doctrine: The Rise of Disaster Capitalism.* (New York: Picador, 2008) 271.

4. "15 Years after `IMF Crisis'" Koreatimes. November 20, 2012. Accessed October 19, 2016. http://www.koreatimes.co.kr/www/news/opinon/2013/08/202_125125.html. and "South Korea's Middle Class Is Shrinking, According to Recent Report." English Edition : The Hankyoreh. Accessed October 15, 2016. http://english.hani.co.kr/arti/english_edition/e_business/678354.html.

trillion won to 911 trillion won. Many South Koreans saw the IMF as an occupational force annexing the country. A more cynical, but realistic view, is that the IMF crisis was just a turn in America's neo-imperial project, not only in South Korea, but Asia at large. The continued occupation of 100,000 American troops stationed in the region serve a dual function, as the historian Bruce Cummings has written, they act to both contain the enemy and constrain the ally. Hence the totalitarian order that lives beneath the so-called freedom of liberal "democracy" became suddenly visible when the economy cracked in 1997.

The children are silently having a snowball fight with their eyes. The snow is just the cover. Fights always contain hard rocks at their core.

Kim Haengsook,
"Memories Collect When No One is Noticing"

Many Korean academics have tended to stress the historicity of Korean poetry—voices and works whose words can be tied to specific political and socio-historical periods— poems as "historical records of change through language."[5] This is especially true from postwar poetry of the 1960's to the poetry that accompanied the larger Minjung movement that lead up to democracy in the late 1980's. In an introduction to a collection of the poets,

5. *Kim, Su-yŏng, Kyŏng-nim Sin, Si-yŏng Yi, Anthony, and Yŏng-mu Kim. Variations = Sarang Ŭi Pyŏnjugok. (Ithaca: East Asia Program, Cornell University, 2001) xiii.*

Kim Su-Young, Shin Kyong-Nim, and Lee Si-Young, each representing a different decade from that timespan, Jikwan Yoon writes that the "moral conscience" a poet maintains while under systems of political and social oppression "creates a constant state of crisis" that results in "anguish, resentment, and shame about his life in the present." He makes the very bold declaration that it " is from this [crisis] that true poetry emanates."[6]

> *Dance Dance Revolution!*
> *Whenever I miss a step and stomp your foot to death*
> *Why do you repeatedly call my name?*

Kim Min Jeong, "Red, an Announcement"

From a philosophical perspective, Yoon's observation about "true poetry" proves problematic in several ways. It is a view that privileges history and autobiography over aesthetic determination. Supposing that there is such a thing as a stable "morals" or "conscience," the artistic act is always a reflection or a reaction to forces of history. From this point of view poetry is an artifact for gaining historical knowledge, not a force of historical change. It is reactive rather than revolutionary. When we talk about modern literature in Korea, there are many modernisms, and within each modernism, many histories made up of a dizzying array of voices. The desire for an authentic literature that embodies a historical moment is ultimately a desire to flatten the diversity of voices that pay witness to multi-lived

6. *Kim, Su-yŏng xiii-xiv.*

experiences. Indeed, that desire has tended to privilege a traditional male voice, while silencing outsiders.

Even though *Miraepa* is widely believed to be an incongruous movement behind a label, that there is no aesthetic thread to bind poets of that generation together, I believe such incongruity is a reflection of how it is not contemporary art, but lived reality that has become unbound from the historical narrative of the nation and its literature. There is not one Korea, not one way of being Korean, and not one way of being a woman in Korea. From an aesthetic level, perhaps the thing that binds these three poets, and many poets of this generation, is a rejection of the kind of authentic subjectivity that produces "true poetry." Like Yi Sang's anti-hero[7] who spreads wings which are fake, the work of these poets ask us what is morality in an amoral world, what is political freedom when the future is bought? In liberal democracy there is the freedom to vote, the freedom to choose, but the power of choice becomes an empty gesture in a political and economic reality that is pre-figured.

Awake, I am Desdemona, Patzzi, Annabelle Lee, the Barideki
Living reality in an exceptional time without dreams—

Kim Yi Deum, "More than Aura, Aori"[8]

---

7. The narrator who spreads his "imitation wings" on top of the Mitsukoshi department store in the infamous final scene in the story "The Wings." see Yi, Sang, Chŏng-hyo An, James B. Lee, Sang Yi, Sang Yi, and Sang Yi. *The Wings.* Seoul: Jimoondang Pub., 2001.
8. Kim I-dŭm. *Hisŭt'eria: Kim I-dŭm Sijip.* (Sŏul: Munhak Kwa Chisŏngsa, 2014). (The translation is mine)

Over this past summer I said in an interview for Kyung Han news that Korea should nominate a woman poet for the Nobel Prize. I think women's poetry, because it has always been pushed to the margins, is written outside the historical lens of male "authenticity," that it best embodies the chaos of contemporary life. I think the reason recent narratives written by Korean women, poetry written by Korean women, and films depicting Korean women have resonated so heavily with audiences outside of Korea is because, in one of the most patriarchal countries on earth, women have been pioneers of a culture that is powerfully apart, unstable, and unrooted from the "official" national narrative. As Don Mee Choi wrote in an introduction to the pioneering collection of poetry written by Korean women *Anxiety of Words*, women poets use "unconventional forms of language" to develop a style of poetry that is "unreal, surreal, and even fantastical" as a form of resistance and survival to that culture of oppression. Following in the tradition pioneered by Kim Hyesoon, Choi Seung Ja, and Yi Yon-ju, Kim Yi Deum's poems burst with an excess of bodily fluids that undo the social and political silencing of the female body, performing what Ruth Williams called the "revolutionary grotesque," while Kim Min Jeong destabilizes gender constructs by exposing the often funny and contradictory rifts that appear in the language of everyday circumstance. Both use slang, punning, cultural referents, and 'naughty, unwomanly' language in order to challenge readers to expand their ideas of not only what a poem is, but also how women should speak. Kim Haengsook uses geospatial transformation in order to project her inner-life into a communal, shared landscape. Like a cubist, she moves geographically, catching multiple perspectives of subjects lived in a singular time, but trapped in a two dimensional space. In their own way each author undermines patriarchal authority by displaying the absurd and illogical nature of gender expectations. But even larger than issues of gender, these poems reveal the illogical systems of power behind the apparent structures that govern the logic of everyday life. By making the source of these antagonisms and gender transgressions visible, they make them less powerful, less terrifying.

The poets and poems included in this collection speak to the tumultuous period of the last 15 years. However, that does not mean that we should read them as a definitive representation of their generation (all three are just now entering their mid-career), or even as symbolic of all contemporary poetry being written in Korea, but instead as a small sample of the diversity of contemporary Korean literature that has yet to become available to an English speaking audience.

Jake Levine (2016)

KIM YIDEUM

Translated by
Jiyoon Lee, Johannes Göransson, and Don Mee Choi

A GROWN-UP

He looks at the photo of a hobo's corpse which was
donated to the hospital as a cadaver. She was probably a
mental patient without a family. You should stop drifting
too. That's also an illness, he says while he strokes me. He
rubs oil all over my body. Then he tightens and loosens
me. Your problem is that you are always out of control.
Let's gently and slowly go for a long, long ride. Empty out,
pause, and empty out, only then you're visible. Actually,
let's just go out for quick one. His voice is always strange,
sly, and beautiful.

But I'm already outdated. I'm too big – I can't be folded
or transported.

I barely make it through the dried-up pond. There's a lost-
and-found building. The Green Party built it. I put a chain
around his long neck. I don't touch any of his bike bling.
I balance myself against the rack. I need a breather. Do I
need a lock? As long as you stay tied up, I'm not going
anywhere. The bicycle parade is over, and I jeer at my
exhausted self from speeding down the bike lane, I jeer at
my idiotic self for trying so hard.

Yesterday, I signed up for organ donation. I felt like
speeding away with an empty basket hanging from my

handle bars—it was that kind of an afternoon. I had the urge to kill somebody for no reason at all.

And for no reason at all, I wonder what time it is. My seat and handles have been torn off and one of the wheels is missing. My soul, like a flat tire, is hanging from the bike rack. In these dark times, I keep my feet on the ground together with the rest of the abandoned bikes. I stop. What am I seeing? I open the tool-box and try to mend my shredded soul. My wet shoulders. Another bike thief approaches. He caresses me. Then he pisses on my bent spokes, wheels. I shake my pedals as if I'm about to take off in a frenzy.

THERE IS A WORD GHOST

Singers vanish like the songs they sing
Words become seeds
The graffiti artist I liked suddenly perished
like the words he scrawled on the back-alley wall
Not that everything works that way

What if my words randomly become a song?
What if they carry me off?

When I was into eclectic music, extreme kisses, and silent
    movies
In other words, when I thought I was a grown-up
I hung out with people who doubted words and songs,
intent on bashing them as if they were betting on
whether someone trapped under a bulldozer would live or not

But on a quiet day like today
I hear the sound of the dead breathing
from everywhere, anywhere. How is it possible?

I need to speak now or never,
for the intensity of guilt is slowly fading.

I thought I wouldn't get pregnant if he pulled out.
The future is already set.

Please don't grow!
Please fall out!
I ride on the back of a motorcycle, doing crazy shit,
thinking, please get out of my body, get out, get out!

A storm of bloody water explodes, leaks, spreads.
Your knees are cut, your ankles are cut in my vagina.
Look at your tennis shoes!
It looks like red paint has been spilt on the road.
Please stop me.
Don't leave me in here

If you'd died like I said
before you were pulled out of my body with tweezers
before you were cut with scissors
would millions of red birds have fallen? Gravity.
Would I have sung about the tragic scene I had scraped out?
If not for gravity
who could say a word about it? Who could've said a word
    about it?

Tonight I am drunk.
I keep breaking broken instrument again and again.
No more hesitation or torment.

The smell of the scented candle returns
in this hour when I fall into a swamp covered in leaves
like a drunken killer who has beautifully staged her own
    confession.

I don't know what I should say
what my words have done
Oh, I will say it again, I loved your words, that's is all.
I'm drooling.
Drip, drip, drip, the words melt.
Hey, you, shove my saliva back into my mouth.

DAYDREAMS OF A POND

I'm sitting across from the oldest, biggest, fattest man I have ever seen. He looks like has been sitting on a tatami mat with his mouth open in a dark basement for twenty years. A noodle bowl, a bible, cigarettes, a knife, a mask, and colorful medicine bottles are scattered on the blackish shelf above his grey head. The dark sauce from the tipped-over Worcestershire bottle drips down on his gloomy, almost-dead face.

A lot of things have changed since last year when I first arrived here. The man has become much fatter and quieter. Back then, a disgusting odor spread from the guest house and Mozart's Fugue in C major, K.394 rippled out. Who would be crazy enough to walk up the super slippery hill and knock on the squeaky door of the cabin? Already back then, he looked over a hundred years old and must have weighed at least 330 pounds, and if he were to stand up straight, his head would touch the ceiling. "Well, thank you very much," the mice squeaked as I twirled up pasta around my fork and shoved it in his mouth. The cabin remained dark even though the moonlight was seeping in, and the decrepit heater, the litters of mice and the steam from our breaths created a chaotic ambience.

Even upon close examination he was not handsome: When he smiled, the wrinkles in his face looked like rat tails. All the same, I couldn't help smiling as I watched him fill up the tub with water for his grubby guest. He moved like a corpse.

After leaving him, I cried and cried all the way down the snow-covered hill. I handed a ticket to the train conductor as I wiped my tears, and since then my cheeks have never once been wet with tears. I sneered and shrugged, but I still came back to him a year later. He said that we needed to find the mountain. "Well, take a look! There's no mountain called Mount Toe, is there?" He watched me quietly for a while. His face, twisted like a Francis Bacon portrait, turned gray like ink stone. Last year, he insisted that Rosa Luxemburg was the name of a cyclone, then he went on for nearly two hours about how art couldn't be distinguished from the righteousness of celestial bodies. There never was such a storm. The cyclone didn't exist.

I raised my hand to shoo off a bug. I stretched out on the floor. I didn't know how my hair got soaked. I looked around. Outside the window, a cloud passed by that looked like a boulder, and there was a big tree next to the boulder, which turned into a bird and then an elephant. I'm going to take off to Madagascar to see the baobab trees. But where the heck is Mount Toe? He's never been there, but he's always overcome by the feeling that he'd been back and forth. Does this mountain really exist somewhere?

The evening darkness approaches the guest hut at the edge of the hill, where one can sit and look at the pond. The old man falls asleep, and I think about all the things I rejected after being kicked out of my sanctuary, how I rebelled against everything I longed for. Oh, this thick head of mine always seeks contradictions! Oh, I love things that run away, things that disappear! At night, with ear buds on, I mumble to myself, "Mozart had lived too long." Then I become ecstatic like a stirred-up pond as I recall the pianist who said in his last hour that he wanted to spend a winter in the dark and cold of the Arctic.

"If you don't do it soon, you'll never do it. You'll just end up doing something else." In the middle of the night, a fat hand reaches up to my bed. The hand opens the piano lid. His trembling fingers strike the keys without hesitation. My stiff joints ache until his extremely sensitive touch create pleasurable sounds. I watch him with my eyes closed. Will I ever cry again? He won't be here next year. In this fleeting moment, perhaps we share the friendship of a lifetime through the mere touching our fingertips.

I cut his tangled hair. I leave alone his beard and wash the rest of his face. He just keeps his arms crossed and gazes out at the overcast sky while I put shoddy socks on his filthy feet. Then I dress him in a wool sweater, pull leather gloves on his hands, and prop him up outside. He clings to my shoulder the way a shipwrecked person clings a wooden plank in an icy storm. We may be heading toward

Mount Toe. His dim eyes squint with joy. His drooling mouth opens and closes but makes no sound. He's like his broken piano, which had been in a repair shop for nearly seven years. He takes two steps and falls with a loud thud. "How fast can you go?" I hop on his belly. With a cruel smile I touch him as if it were the end or the beginning of the world. There will be a perfect swirl drawn here with his chest as the axis. We drive our bodies down the hill. We cross fear. Through the detour we'll arrive at the essence. There's no gear that regulates our speed, so we adjust our speed by rubbing our bodies against the undulating hill. By the time we are almost all the way down, the dizzying variations are over, and we no longer know if our spiraling bodies are going up or down. You have to see this place if your body wants to reach the destination before your slow mind. Because he stopped here, this banal pond becomes significant.

His name is on the tip of my tongue. His devastatingly beautiful face is completely ruined from the time he got into a car wreck trying to pass another car. At first, I couldn't even shake his hand, afraid that he was infectious. This washed-up pianist, who claims he found music after he stopped singing and playing, is stubborn. He makes me stand in front of a strange-looking tree—it's not even a baobab tree—and takes a photo. Soon, he takes my hand and walks me across the frozen pond. We pass several holes in the ice. I fall down on the ice, exhausted. I lie on my stomach. I stretch out my arms and pull the chain up from the hole. A frozen girl who is covering her face comes up with the chain. "A murder took place right under your feet and all the fleshy fruits have rotted. Beware of the Toe." Oh my god, I awake from the dark, deep sleep, but I can't see anything. It's early dawn. What about the old man and the girl? Where did my trees, my fists, and my chain go? I can't shake off this unbearable feeling of time and space being out of sync. I crouch, pressing my ears against the thin ice. The scared mice are squeaking, and I hear the old man coughing and the door creaking. Two secretive eyes, molded together in the center, peer at me. I'm engulfed in pain as if I'm being skinned from neck to knees. These inner vibrations can destroy mountains, these meaningless coincidences—how long will they last?

ANNA O'S OFFICE

I'm glad we built this house right next to the beach. At
night, I can hear the waves crash just outside the balcony.
You're pitch-black, and your gown is perfectly white.
How did you come all the way up here? Did you come
here alone? I'm impressed! I like things that I can flip
through, then toss, like the magazine I brought from the
Sorbonne. Great, great! The way you undress in a hurry,
flipping your orange hair, is so painful to watch that I
have to hug you. Hehehe. We fly high above the clouds
without smashing the ceiling. You stare at me, even before
we land, like a dead rabbit next to a radiator. Want me
to hold you again? Want to die with a hard-on? Want
something to eat? Hehe. Well done! You packed a to-go-
box of lettuce and gourmet French sausages. Never mind,
just suck on my tits. You'll get anxious as if struck by some
unbelievable idea. Oh my, you sound like a white noise
machine. Uhuhuh. Stop making that sound. Want to do it
again? Want to try holding your breath till you can hear
the small waves and the plastic bag flapping against the
cracked window? Gasp gasp. You're the one who's stabbing
me, in and out, so why are you acting like you're the one
dying? Like a toothbrush, like feathers stuffed in a sleeping
bag, so thinly padded, I'll roll your little head, littler than
a pupil, around and around in my mouth. Ahahah. Stop!
I love you! I've heard all this till before, my ears have

grown callused. All my life, my lovers have sent me letters scribbled like horrible subtitles in translation, then they all throw themselves into the ocean. Are you getting nervous? You're holding me so tight. Do you want to go back? I'm busy, I don't have time for a break. It's time to close up the office. Squeeze it all out, at least six times, on my belly, in my hands. When I opened the window, it was hailing, to my surprise. This won't do. Would it make you happy if I take a nibble of your chewy thing? Come on, wake up! You and me, facing the blazing wind. Anyway, who can see us, shouting and flying, scattering a flurry of semen? They'd think it was a hallucination of a ghost licking cheese soup. Is your nose bleeding? Have you stopped breathing? Oh, I'll kiss you, so there's no chance of you coming back to life any time soon. Take a nap and come back tomorrow at two. I promise, it will be thrice as fun. I'll praise your dirty thoughts, your endless depression. Anyway, I wonder if my favorite patient, Sigmund, will ever show up?

WHILE THE GERMOPHOBIC
MAN WASHES UP

After you've gone into the bathroom to wash up, I look
in the mirror. I slowly take my clothes off. I crouch in
the corner of the bed to avoid the excessive gaze of
the mirror. I get up and go to the kitchen. I open the
refrigerator and drink water.

While you're washing up, I turn on the radio and look
vacantly out the window at the deserted street.

Are you almost done?
I'm still washing myself.

I look at your watch, put on your glasses, flip open your
cellphone. I open your closet and count your neatly hung
white shirts.

Is it the countless germs, or the unspeakable feeling of
filthiness, or is it the soap foam that makes you wash
yourself over and over? Fine, keep washing yourself until
there's nothing left, until your face is all gone, totally
mangled.

I drink some coffee, pick a book from the shelf and read
it. The books weren't randomly shelved. I start to read a

book about maintaining hygiene with a terrifying level of order and control. The preface is too long. I was going to have another cup of coffee, but instead I go for a beer, an overflowing beer.

I get naked and let everything hang, sideways, without shame. It's like I'm at a nude beach. I hurl the shitty book about sanitary science and preventive medicine across the room. I'm impure, I grow more and more obscene.

I write, write, write the way you wash.

Hey, are you done washing yet?
No, the soap won't rinse off, the water pressure is too weak.

I bet you'll never come out of the bathroom because when you touch the door-knob, you'll have to wash again. You'll want to get near me, but you won't touch me. You'll wash. You'll want to stop, but you'll just keep washing yourself over and over again. You'll become contaminated, you'll go on dying, and you'll have to wash again, regardless of the time of day or night.

A lifetime. If such a thing remains between us, you will wash and I will write. I'll rip up the paper, then write again, keeping a door between us.

We wait obsessive-compulsively for each other to not appear.

DECEMBER

I like that it's evening now.
I like standing on the street
watching things grow blurry
watching pedestrians pass by, trembling under their coats.
I like watching their neckless faces.
I like waiting for you.
I won't be able to finish today's round of affirmations and
    self-shaming.
I'm leaving it all unfinished.
I'm proud of my ability to run toward the goal line just
    to quit.
The trees have done their best to shed their leaves.
A flock of birds flap their wings desperately
flying off in different directions.

I'm happy that it's winter, not spring.
It's not a new year, it's the end of the year, and I'm totally
    fucked up.
How nice that it isn't the first time.
Soon I won't even be able to make out your body.
You, my lover with your deep-socketed eyes and pale skin.
Get up, lets go to my room.
Are you just going to stand around and drink
water like it's a funeral,
or can we mess around one last time?

Are you taking your last breath? Dear Soulmate,
what did you ever do for me anyway?

CONSTRUCTION CONTRACTOR

I insist that the wall shouldn't be smashed. I will finish removing the non-load-bearing walls and begin the remodeling. Get the hell out or go kill yourself. I worked naked and the feminist professor labored in a petticoat. He or she preferred frosted glass windows. I flew about like a brick, and the bourgeois feminist professor hit the painter: "That's not how it was in the floor plan. Put it in the can." His or her door was so complicated that it had to be pushed down then rotated and then pushed back up. But I just wanted to be done with the job: "How do you expect me to remodel this crazy place? I shouldn't have hired you guys." I just needed a new, unreasonable living space that can be shared by three people. I charged at the wall. "You think this is the way it's done? No this is how it's done. Give me break, do you get it?" If I would have understood this tedious remodeling process, if I would have stayed in charge of the wrecking of the walls, if I could have figured out the whole thing, I wonder if we would have finished this boring job tonight.

RESTORATION OF SILENCE

1.

The soldier disappeared three days before, and the three
brothers died one after another. She was on her way
to cram school, after leaving the alley noodle shop. She
hugged the wall to avoid the sparks from the foundry.
The familiar welder brothers and their friend in the army
outfit tied up the girl and raped her for two days straight,
pouring cold water on her so they could all get a share of
the scraps. One of the men lifted a shiny hammer above
the forehead of the girl, or what was left of her, and a
metal fireball from heaven struck right above the down-
casted whites of her eyes.

2.

A case without a witness gets swept under the rug, and
people say they'll get what they deserve in the end, the
truth will come out. No, it won't. The truth is heading
toward annihilation. I'm the ultimate ideal but I'm made
of flesh and blood.

When the sand beneath my feet becomes soggy, I sneak
out of the fortress and walk past the shore scattered

with dead birds. I pass the forest trail where the clouds look like torn-up, blood-stained sanitary napkins. I pass fingers addicted to triggers, gallows draped with masks, the laughter of rapists, and the ground-shaking march of soldiers. I giddily hop over the giddy border. I can hear the sound of the camera shutter of the bourgeois, feminist documentary filmmaker. Why does it sound so sexy?

Ahahah, please just go away. Don't stir things up. Those wryly funny things, those things that I have forgotten for now, let those things pass. Those things spilling out from the memories branded in our brains, from the restored paintings, from the cemetery on the bare mountain, 600 meters above sea level. Impossible. I see them as an amalgamation, but it's an illusion. One year ago today, my file of poems vanished without a trace. I hope the contract I made with the devil doesn't get renewed.

3.

Samurai warriors contemplate how they'll die, and a younger student from my school who doesn't know who I am receives an award. Actually, I don't know who he is either. The author of *Slaughterhouse-Five* and *Cat's Cradle* is going to die in a week. The Bob from Bob Dylan, the Ben from Ben Morrison—it's so hard to separate the names. I'm sick of them all. Poetry readings are boring. I won't reveal the younger student's name—I'm also sick of myself. You call yourself Kim Yideum, but are you a hundred percent sure you're Yideum? Tell her to fuck off. Don't put on that corny act. Why don't you go ahead and sing yourself? I lean back for a moment, so I won't get dried fish flakes on the laptop, and scarf down a bland veggie dish. While I am at it, I scarf down the unwieldy spoon and chopsticks too. I even nonchalantly read the poems that the young poet won't have time to write before she is strangled to death, at exactly 6 pm, while the northwest wind blows. Nobody will listen to me read the poems, even if I act all crazy.

4.

How hilarious that my family salutes, no, bows to the back of my cracked skull. Their eyes twitch. They sit in a circle like metal pipes welded together against their will. They throw my leftover veggies into a large bowl and mix them up. While I rub my eyelids and roll the metal ball back and forth, my father comes into my room and crouches on top of my knees. He strokes his penis with one hand for a while. Why is he touching my laptop with his unwashed grubby hand? Maybe it has a virus? Or did that bitch delete everything before she croaked? Maybe I can make some money if I recover the files and put together a posthumous collection.

AT THE LABORATORY

With a clear mind, I get right into the experiment.
I put on my lab coat and scrub my hands with
foamy soap all the way up to my wrists.
I cut out the tongue from a dead bird
and I tear out the swim bladder from a dead fish
and I escape from the birth canal of my dying mommy.

With a clear mind, I read a book.
This page doesn't line up with the word "mother" from
    the previous page,
but the fragmented words line up according to a different logic.
When spring arrives, the black-headed goldfinch takes off
    to Siberia.
For the past two years, I've been tracking his migratory route.
Some birds can't find their way home by themselves,
but they can't blend into the flock either,
so nobody will notice that he'd vanished.
Free from relationships, I take off.

He had a short tongue and spoke in complicated sentences.
He always omitted the subject
and I especially had a hard time noticing
the subtle differences between prepositions.

When I discovered the groundbreaking method
through which I could understand him,
I was horrified and burnt down the basement lab.

With a clear mind, I sing.
I hope the final chorus will drag away the lead vocalist and
    shred his voice.
From start to finish, there's been nothing noble or vile about
    this poem.
The birds and the fish were rotten, and the multi-colored
    flowers were repulsive.
I know for sure who my mommy is – she's the one on the
    shelf – but who was he?
His fingerprints look like Daddy's.
They produce a bountiful crop in the cold darkness.
I collect frozen piss.

I want to go outside, but Mommy's not pushing hard enough
The co-worker yells, If the wings of the nose show, use the
    forceps to pull it out!
They wipe the kitten's mouth and ears with gauze.
Rosy cheeked, I gaze into the mirror, blushing.
I slurp up a bowl cream with meds mixed in.
It clears up my mind.

THE MAY OF GOYA AND ME

Kim Yideum and Francisco Goya talk about The Second
of May, they stitch themselves together and pour water
into their ears, Mother whines and cries, "Help me"
inside my ear, senile Napoleon speaks with a lisp and
deaf Goya collapses next to the severed head of a horse,
I glance at the illustrated guide to pit vipers (which has
no nothing to do with the Spanish Revolution), a no-
name public health doctor cuts open a patient's belly for
a caesarean then hides her face when she dies from his
hack-job...

Most art pathologists claim that The Second of May can't
be moved. I've been in labor since this morning. Actually,
I've been in labor for decades. "I'm so tired, Mother!"
They say Goya's The Third of May can't be moved.
Yideum from the Third of May, here, have some milk, I
don't understand a word of what you're saying.

They say bombs went off and Madrid was blown up when
her water broke.
Is there anything else you want blown up?
The soldier probably deserted his post in order to go
strangle his lover.
They say the deaf old man at the end of the hallway in the
hospital room, the single mother, the orphan all died from

severe blood loss. It's so obvious that I had nothing to do with my birth.

Goya can go outside but not the Second of May.

It's because we want to preserve it, there's no way around it. Mother's Second of May deteriorated so badly I was not allowed to identify it.

All these things are completely unrelated. Do you want me to yoke them together?

You wanted to rot faster, so you changed the temperature, humidity and lighting.

If I'd known the conditions for proper deterioration were going to be the same conditions as for survival, I wouldn't have collected all these things associated with Mother.

Mother is lying in the middle of my room, which is like a showroom for junk.

Look, she's over there, lying on my bed. Now we won't be able to get rid of any of these things because she's stinking up the room. Today happens to be my birthday and she's playing dead!

THE ARIA FROM THE RICE CHEST

If I hide here nobody will be able to find me,
not even my sister or Daddy.
I tear the moon's mask off.
This moon can't even fake a smile.
I call her Mom, then throw up the rice she feeds me.
The rice worms haven't rotted.
In the moonlight, swarming moths have
devoured half of the rice chest that is my body.
Oh, my head sticks out.
I don't want to get caught.
I'll be calm, calm from now on.
So please don't' make a stew out of my head!
Oh, I will call you Mother!
She still has a basket of flesh left over
after eating a heap of boiled meat.
Chunks have scattered everywhere.
Now the rice chest enters the skull
and sings out.
An aria of joyous screams.
A flopping tongue.
The bones of white trees on the moon.
They waver, waver.

KIM MIN JEONG

Translated by
Jiyoon Lee and Jake Levine

FINALE

As the belt tightened around my neck
I merely stared
So he up and left.

As the poet might treat a chicken,
He could eat me
But he couldn't slaughter me
Because he was such a delicate man.

And today
My right hand that I gave to him
By thrusting it in his back pocket
Has suddenly returned.

Both long and wide, the right palm has grown
3 centimeters in size
Bigger than the left. And the nails!
Well trimmed like cones good for juicing
Beneath the hot, orange-plumping sun.

They were perfect for
Popping the fleshy pimples that thrust up willy nilly
After I scraped off the chicken skin,
So I forgot the itty bitty death in me.

Yeah, that's how I shake it.
Say hello to the new me!

BUTTERFLY ADDICT

On the road home
I saw a girl carrying a milk cow over her shoulder.
Someone who also wants to drink milk. I can relate.

With stockings on my feet, I return to the farm.
You are gone and
I fear the milk cow udders left unsuckled
are too many for me to handle alone.
While each knife stab and fork poke softens the blood soaked
    tablecloth

like the nectar of a fleeting butterfly
peeing its pants in secret, urine

is always a repeating sign, a sonic outro
like the last puff of the breath of a fish
on its way to death.

Hanging on the clothesline, leather from a milk cow flaps and
I swear, until the rechargeable battery of my tongue's base is
    completely drained,
I will lick the loins of the milk cow's back with the quivering
    tip of my tongue.

Decalcomania, stay-wet.

UNMARRIED AND FORTY*

I said Hagik-dong, but when I got out of the taxi and looked around the road, I was in the middle of Kkik-dong. *Is it that easy to say? Yeah, that damn easy.* Just like the darkness that fattened for forty years. And the shadier it did, the more scarlet bright the courtyard of the "Yellow House" shone. The day before his enlistment, my father's virginity surrendered. It got buried here. Now I wonder, is it still possible to dig it up? I look back. Mom who turned into a rock pleads earnestly, *Don't look back.* About to pick up the *Introduction to Literature* book that fell to the ground, my eyes run into my Kkik-dong older sister, who, poking her high heel into a page of the book puts it like this: *What are you looking at cunt? Aren't you just another of those Inha Uni whores?* On verdant lawns on the main road to campus in Hagik-dong, the Kkik-dong older sisters are laid out like a blanket, chewing gum, smacking their gums, slapping down Hwatu cards. If they are tickled to death by the stares of girl students passing by, they grab the washbasin for cleaning vaginas and splash it at those students. *The fucking bitches,* and before the water from the washbasin for cleaning vaginas on the ground dries, they spit, but as they do, the busily spitting throats of the Kkik-dong older sisters get dry. Thirsting for something different, even to spit phlegm is a waste of moisture, so as the days pass they keep their throats shut like silent gravel.

Girls, when you are wearing sailor costumes and grabbing the arms of randoms in the street, save your sweat beads. However, like pots of kimchi, I wonder if you will ever learn how to get off your backs? One day when I said Kkik-dong to the driver and I got dropped out of the taxi outside a newly built Hagik-dong apartment, I guess I realized that all I ever needed to do to get there was cross the street.

*Kkik-dong is just another name for Hagik-dong, a university street, but also refers to the area known for prostitution.

TITS NAMED DICK

You've got dick,
And I've got tits, however
Let's not make it a spectacle.
If you think that's childish
Remember it's from you where things got started.

Anyway, a point we share is that when we grab, we hold one ha
Anyway, a point we share is that when we suck lips, we suck
    one set.
Anyway, a point we share is that when we chop, we use one p

(Ah, they scooped out one of my cancerous tits. What harsh
    equality, the dizzying relief.)

After splitting the sex up
Dos-a-dos, we sleep
In the direction of our respective hearts, like donuts,
Really like do-ugh-nuts, curling heavily atop the bed
Vastly cast

Two sets of breasts
Two balls

How lovely!

PENIS NAMED FACE

What an extremely obvious story

I try to draw a circle because I miss you, but carelessly
I draw a squishy faced bread twisty. If the bread twisty's
deliciousness is delicious, the banana's banana-ing is long,
and if the banana's banana-ing is long, the train's train-ing
is slow, and that slowness is stretchy-ing, a stretchy-thing,
a bread twisty.... All the day long, even if I am a person
I do not understand, throwing the twisty bread ballad fit,
even if the illusion is more uterus than moneyless, more
ovulation-time than hunger-time, finally I am freed! To
The Twisty Bread Inn! No, the Twisty Bread Motel—I
mean I'm not serious. I don't really want to get a room.
I'm just wondering, do you think the Twisty Bread
business was named by a woman or a man?

So the story is really banal

Now, even though I can't recall his face, the pants he shit
hanging above his ankles remain so vivid in my mind. I
could have bought you a belt .... Why didn't you tell me
how hot the kettle mouth boiled? If I had known, I would
have blown to cool it down .... In this world there are
two crimes that need to be unconditionally forgiven. One
is being young. The other is being deaf. Surrounded by
silence, you and I were in a car backing up, and Jesus hung
with a rubber band to the rearview mirror was bobbing

up and down. I guess that's why they say, *a beautiful crime is always caused by love.*

And yet, it's a story I'll never get sick of

Yesterday we went to a Tous-Les-Jours coffee shop because the actor Jo In-Sung said we should. And today we went to a Dunkin Donuts coffee shop because the actor Lee Sun Kyun said we should. This pastry, that pastry, this twisty bread, that twisty bread . . . . *how do people live on that bread shit? It all tastes like the same shit.* Our Boss Sister said that. And she was so right.

RED, AN ANNOUNCEMENT

RED SHOES

I wore the red shoes you bought me for the first time.
With my lover who you know, I went to the arcade.
Dance Dance Revolution!
Whenever I miss a step and stomp your foot to death
Why do you repeatedly call my name?
With a lowered glance, you are standing there
At the welcome counter of the arcade,
The hand exchanging coins.

Sorry. I'm in the middle of an affair!

RED PANTIES

Right after my lover who you know made his confession
Eli Eli Lema Sabachtani!
You said let's just hold hands and go to sleep.
Even though you snored and I could have swore you fell
    into a dream
Why do you repeatedly call my name?
Underneath my red panties, I am wearing a white winged
    tampon and
Because I sat on the toilet in the bathroom too long, my
    ass is numb.

Sorry. I'm having my period!

RED RADISH

You asked me, what the hell is this swelling desire?
Because he was married and impotent
My lover, who you know, was an absolutely lovely man.
a hundred miles, a hundred miles ... ...
you've got to say it three more times, to five hundred
    miles, and yet
why is it that you continually call my name?
Without wearing clothes, I went outside to grab the
    morning paper and
Made eye contact with the man who is my next door
    neighbor
Who, let's face it, was a red radish I bit into.

Sorry. I am eating!

GIRL-DOT-COM

Girl.
Wave perm, or is it
A cheap-ass wig?
Girl.
Heavy makeup, or is that
A peachy fuzz face.
Girl.
Boob King,
With shrunken shoulders.
Girl.
Wearing an itty bitty mini-skirt
With the *FRESH* icy-hot
Patching her thigh.
Girl.
Or not?

THAT WOMAN FEELING,
FOR THE FIRST TIME

It was at Cheonnan station.

Waiting for the last train, delayed, alone.

I heard the *tok tok* of somebody killing lice.

But where did the noise come from?

On the platform, a homeless man clipping his nails.

Beneath a beat army jumper, his panties in the wind.

Through the gap in his crotch, hair dirtily sticking out,
    blackened.

Hey girl, it's so damn cold, can you just give me 300 won?

I bought a six-hundred-won Nescafe can and put it in
    front of him.

Hey not that kind. I meant the vending machine. Sweet and big.

I bought a three-hundred-won coffee and put it in front
    of him.

Inside the electric display

a message that the Seoul bound train

was another ten minutes delayed

quickly floated by.

**CONTACT A CHEONNAN PRECINCT STATION
MINISTRY OF WOMEN REPRESENTATIVE: 041-
566-1989**

In that instant, I urgently fumbled for a pen with my hand

through the pocket of my coat and

suddenly I felt the coffee can's warmth.

Oh, is this the feeling of that poem that says
  Spring arrives
  Even if you are not waiting for it
On this night where I read **MINISTRY OF WOMEN** as
  MINISTRY OF REASON.
Or did it say **MINISTRY OF THE OPPOSITE SEX?**★

★In the Korean there is play between 여성 and 이성, where 이성
means both "reason" and "opposite sex".

MY NAME IS NASTY

A poet's book was being printed.
The man on the night time Buddhist program
Said that a Buddhist nun gave him
An expensive fountain pen.
Before the poetry book finished printing
There was a phone call inquiring about the new book.

This is the I Am Temple. I live here. Yes.
I'll take 100 copies.
Here is my address:
Gyeongnam, Secret Sunshine City, Uninhabited County, My
    House #553.
My name is Nasty
And the recipient's name
Is The Nasty Monk.

After the order I exchanged many messages with the
    monk.
If you know Secret Sunshine City, it's probably because of the
    actress Jeon Do-yeon
(the actress in the Secret Sunshine movie)
Anyway, you know I Am Temple, the place where I live?
It's a perfect place for women.

So really, come visit me anytime! texted the monk.

When I think of the monk, the only thing think

Is Nasty, and somehow,

No, the time still doesn't feel quite . . . .

Nope, still not ready.

BEAUTIFUL AND USELESS

Last winter when I went to Uljin in Kyungbok we got a stone
As if plucking an egg from a henhouse, carefully
You snatched the stone.
Side by side, spreading out like a V shaped antennae,
Two crab legs stabbed in the sand, emptied of their meat.
The stone was like the torso of a snowman.
The stone was a rock that hollered *Yahoo!*
I spent a few days watching the stone
Dunked in water in a silver bowl.
And then I spent a few days watching the stone
Laying in a dry silver bowl.

It was ink, it was white,
It was night, it was day, and
Like splitting an apple, I always thought it was a blade that cuts
Time into halves, but really it is the stone.
Whenever you needed it, the stone was thrown like a fist!
But never thrown at you, because it was a stone
You chewed.
Like the chin that no longer needs the blade,
Stroke the dull manliness of a stone so long
It could spurt juice.

But even at our peak,
Our juices are juices that never spurt. Isn't that right?

Wash, wash,
As you lathered the stone in soap you said
It doesn't matter how many times it washes,
Water never recognizes the faces of the dead.
So what's the point?
I placed the stone on the lid of the airtight container
Covering the seaweed to
Keep the sea steam from flying out.

When I think of the time we butted heads
To discuss the many utilities of this stone, in retrospect
That was love.

FAREWELL SCENE

We were boy and girl so we slept our sleeps together.
One room.
Two beds.
Three socks.
(When the girl blew her nose she used a sock instead of a han
    Probably.)
The sleeps were tranquil because they were odd numbered an
The sleeps didn't come if they had cold feet.
But to be awake, that is even colder.
Who will go to the desk to check out?

The bill that stacked for three days,
it explodes, now, in a wink.

SHE DID IT ANYWAY

Writing it, casting the net out to sea
Until it's read as lost sheep
It cannot help but be
Infertile, condemned.
I say Love,
A Love that rides the winds of May,
A Love that is Sad, a Sad
Far away.

KIM HAENGSOOK

Translated by
Jiyoon Lee and Jake Levine

THE (DIS)APPEARING PATH

I am walking the same path in different places. Perhaps the path is like a car parked and left temporarily on a roadside. I keep running into the same man in different places.

I am chasing the path. I almost say hello again to the same man. This happened multiple times. Every time it happens, I feel like yellow phlegm is going to jump out my throat. I keep looking back behind me.

Every time I look back, the path disappears like a car's exhaust. The roadside trees are dragged by the path, their scattered leaves are already smooshed. This city has so many people.

When the path disappears, this city turns into a city I've never been to. I have no relatives here, so I sleep at the inn. How strange to not feel like I've lost the path. I'm sick of walking.

I think about how the people who freeze to death on the roadside feel. Again, like a car, the path angrily honks. It's a sound I hear far too often.

A CRYING CHILD

Crying children can't be calmed. I cry and cry until the
inside of my skull is rolling with waves.
If the children won't calm me down, I will . . . the
children . . . they could drown.

Children have no fear, I promise. Look, they sing
underwater. *Mother . . . mother . . . mother . . .* they mouth
like breathing fish.

The bubbles that rose to the surface are popping one after
another. The air stabs them like thorns. Children playing
in the water, they lose track of time.

A NOT-CRYING CHILD

It is so quiet here. The sniffling inside my skull stopped, and
the snot trickling out of my nose froze.
Gak, a sound of something being swallowed whole
splits the silence apart. The following silence is sound asleep.
Is what I feel just the aftershock?
I guess the children really did drown in their sleep. Inside my
skull is a daycare. I need to prepare the blankets to cover up
the children's nightmares.

The children's nightmares are like cars that jump out from
a street corner—hard to dodge. The car drove through me.
How am I supposed to be buying bean sprouts and tofu now?
A child who doesn't cry anymore is dangerous, and despite
the silence,
the snow that falls quietly leaves the village stranded. If
nobody heard of the village,
what would happen then?

I SEE THE 5 AM

The 5 AM street is marvelous. The 5 AM light is blue.
At 5 AM I am not a person who rides a bike.
I am not a person who walks about and mixes her mouth-
exhaust into the 5 AM street.
The 5 AM street is marvelous. The running man drops a
stack of paper and
there is no one to trample it.
The movement of the man collecting scattered papers
slows down. No one is there to chase him.
At 5 AM the man cries. The 5 AM light is blue.
At 5 AM the street lamps aren't turned off yet. At 5 AM I
am not a person who reads the news.
At 5 AM I am not the person on the balcony with her
pajamas fluttering in the air.
On the 5 AM street the man is not a person who squats
and cries. The 5 AM street is marvelous.
The 5 AM light is blue. On the 5 AM street, out of all the
sheets in the all the stacks of paper, not one of them is
crumpled. Not yet.

MEMORIES COLLECT WHEN NO ONE IS NOTICING

Every night I close my eyes. I don't open them for a long time. I don't know what kind of sound will escape if I do. In my life I had just been kicking it around. I don't have any real interests. There is nothing special about me.

Every night I close my eyes and feel the world curl. Just like that, the world changes, I mumble to myself. The roadside trees fall, the road rolls up like a tongue.

Even when the massive animals showed me the rare footage of their mating, nothing became erotic. Dust rose up, blurring my vision. I've never felt interest in another species. Don't assume that I am feeling something just because my eyes are closed.

The children are silently having a snowball fight with their eyes. The snow is just the cover. Fights always contain hard rocks at their core. Their cheeks are swollen red, as if about to burst. The birds, peck, peck, peck their beaks on the field covered white with snow, however,

falling snow fills up the holes fast. The world is still as covered as ever, the holes are deepening. Every night I close my eyes and feel the world getting covered up. That's how things get hidden, and

now that I open my eyes for the first time in a long time, every day I am bewildered. Just like sleep in your eyes, I feel there is something I need to pick.

SANTA SANGRE

—This amount of blood could save at least three people.
—You only care about the quantity of things. This volume of
blood from a nosebleed is impressive, but blood is useless in
this age when all holy superstitions have disappeared.
—from Jodorowsky's *Santa Sangre*

Within the elephant bleeding out of her trunk
there is a baby elephant who is pumping out her blood. *In*
the outside world, what kind of manual labor do people do to reach
death? Mother, I will labor myself to death in my heaven.

The elephant's ears flap. Her enormous body gets baggy.
Mother, we are cleansing together. Your trunk makes a great hose.
Come on, perk up, and spray all around us.

The elephant's blood creates a colosseum. The audience is
gathered by the blood.
Our death-battles are headed in the same direction, so we are at peace.
But, mother, I am still afraid of their orgasms.

Now the elephant's skin drapes saggily. The skeleton that
supports the appearance of the elephant is triumphant.
Mother, it is empty here. I'm a little cold and hungry, but I enjoyed
the labor.
Mother, this place right here, it is still my heaven.

AT THE AGE OF THIRTY

You need the sun shine. The woman put me in a stroller and
we took a walk around the park. *Where is the sun shine? I nee*
something I can touch and play with. I looked up at the woman
The woman also looked up somewhere.

I said *Mother.*
Child, you are just briefly reminiscing about the past, but the world
has changed a lot. The woman released her hands from the gr
of the stroller.

Was it just the wheels that turned? . . . The tree I smashed n
car into arched its back. The leaves, the leaves. I think I heard
the leaves' shrill cackling. *Ah, ah, ah. What is this place that I a*
crammed into?

Love, what's the matter? Disheveled, my love asks. My head is
lodged in the steering wheel. *Where was I headed to? Whereve*
it was, I couldn't stop. I slowly look up at my love.

My love also looks up somewhere. No matter who does it,
anyone looking for an answer looks like an infant. Or was it
really just the wheels that were turning?

I thought, *Mother.* To change directions, first I've got to back u
Slowly I place my hands on the steering wheel. I look back.

THE SCULPTURE GARDEN

A pigeon is sticking its beak between its toes in, out, and
in, repeatedly like a pendulum. I saw its name "Untitled
II" beside its toes. The time was—nod, nod—passing.

A woman was sitting at its side, brushing the grass with
the palms of her hands. Whenever her palm slowly moved,
the grass changed the direction of its body to obey.
Whatever she was thinking, I couldn't see.

THE GOODBYE ABILITY

I am all the things that take gaseous form.
I am cigarette smoke for 2 minutes.
I am rising steam for 3 minutes.
I am oxygen entering your lungs.
I will burn you away with a happy heart.
Did you know that there is smoke billowing from your head?
The meat fat you hate is gently burning
and the intestines became a stovepipe
and the blood boils
and all the birds in the world leave to immigrate,
    commanding the world's fog and

I sing for more than 2 hours
and do the laundry for more than 3 hours
and nap for more than 2 hours
and meditate for over 3 hours
and of course I see the apparitions. They are fucking
    beautiful.
I love you for 2 hours or more,
I love the things that exploded out your head.
Birds snatched the loudly crying children
and took them away.
I learned that in the middle of doing eternal laundry.
My coat turned into a gas.
The thing I pulled out my pocket, a cloud. Your cane.

Well, that's that. In the middle of singing an endless song,
in the middle of taking an endless nap,

there were moments I opened my eyes.
My eyes and ears get clear,
and my Goodbye Ability peaks,
and I shed my fur, and I am cigarette smoke for 2 minutes.
    Rising steam for 3 minutes.
The smell disappears for 2 minutes, and
I take off my clothes. Regarding the clothes dispersing
    into the distant horizon,
regarding my neighbors,
I wave.

HORMONOGRAPHY

O Hormone, light me bright like blazing morning. The Rage is swelling, and I want to manifest it like the eye of a typhoon. That man cheated me. I shall hunt him to the end.

Connected through the milk-lines, I flow to you, I am river Soyang, I am river Nokdong. I am a boatman without an oar. Wherever I end up, if you call me as a man I, as a man, will…

Or if you call me as a woman, I'll try to immerse myself in my role as a woman. From the third, fourth, seventh rung of the ladder between heaven and hell, I'll caress the cards that are dealt to me until I'm destitute. Make me weary. O Hormone, with the gentle caress of your hand, lower the lids of my eyes and

stir up my dreams. I'll be your movie theatre. O Hormone, through big waves stir the landscapes and facial expressions until the screen goes black, until we reach a war-like meaninglessness.

At the mountain spring of the holy hormone, eternally twinkling signals.

TWO CHILDS

When the two childs are playing games, their palms
meeting one another,
The third child…

When the rose vines over the fence are
bang bang blasting rose, rose, rose…

When the two childs are jumping rope, calling out, *come
on in, come inside my home, as if to say we are having fun,*
When the third child is jumping in,
The fourth child…

When an adult is asking, *Dear where is your home?*
The fifth child…
I'm not even born.

Who left this marble behind?
When the marble is changing its color as it is rolling,
when the two childs
chase after the third child until the back alley disappears,

when the two childs look, their eyes meeting one another,
after the back alley completely disappears…
as if to say that was odd.

AN EVEN SMALLER PERSON

I plan to get smaller until I start to get smaller. I am a small person, an even smaller person, a dog, a cat, a single finger, a match.

All my life I stubbornly looked in one direction. All my frowns, scowls, smooshed to wrinkles. Memorable things, light, pain,

after I first breathed, I kept breathing and so my breathe began. Yes, beginnings are like that. The beginning forgets its beginning and the ending doesn't recognize its end and it's no use trying to pronounce mother like the first time and if you say father, oh, my, god!

Once I start to get smaller it begins. I am an even smaller person, an even smaller dog, an even smaller lizard, a small voice, wave interference, a sky without touch,

and the bending wave, the touching raindrop, raindrop, heavier raindrop, I am the shower accompanied by a tornado. Like the world, the umbrellas of small people turned inside out, momentarily stuck to windows, I am the even smaller ripples, inside the window, three children, r*ock, paper, scissors, rock, paper…* making up the rules, making up their roles. One child spreads his palm and tells a mysterious lie about the coin that disappeared

but I couldn't listen to the

THICK RAINBOW

For 3 minutes you tie the laces of your combat boots, and
I am spellbound like tightened feet. When will the war
end? Why are my beliefs offered to decadence? When will
you die? And then when will I?

The thick rainbow under her eyelids rises each day. Do
you believe her? The battlefield is her theme park. Vanity is
the place where she collapses and rises. All her men laced
their combat boots and departed to work.

One day he took off his combat boots and left my side. I
cannot forgive that. Where I am is just 2 kilometers away
from the war zone. Listening to firing guns, children
picnic here in the spring. Why do you think canaries
are yellow and azaleas pink? Why do you vomit red
liquid and why do I let out black water? White powder
falls repeatedly from the sky and the entire city reacts
chemically. Can you believe the color? And the scent?

The woman's convictions take shape as pills dissolve. Don't
believe her too quickly. The chemical reactions she sees are
in excess of standard reality. Futuristic things are decadent.
In her pupils, all that is captured is debris. Dust.

When did you die? And then when did I?

ABOUT THE AUTHORS AND TRANSLATORS

Kim Min-Jeong was born in Inchon in 1976, received a B.A. in creative writing from Chung'ang University and studied at the graduate school of the same university. She made her literary debut in 1999 by winning the Munye chung'ang Rookie Writer's Award. Her publications include *Flying Porcupine Maiden* (2005) and *She Began to Feel - for the First Time*(2009). She is the recipient of the 2007 Pak In-hwan Literary Award.

Kim Yi-Deum has published five books of poetry – *A Stain in the Shape of a Star* (2005), *Cheer up, Femme Fatale* (2007), *The Unspeakable Lover* (2011), *Song of Berlin, Dahlem* (2013), and *Hysteria* (2014), and the novel *Blood Sisters* (2011). Her work has been adapted into a play (*The Metamorphosis,* 2014) and a film (*After School,* 2015). She has received numerous awards for her poetry, including the Poetry & the World Literary Award (2010), the Kim Daljin Changwon Award (2011), the 22nd Century Literary Award (2015) and the Kim Chunsoo Award (2015). She read at the Stockholm International Poetry Festival in 2014 and Biennale Internationale des Poètes en Val-de-Marne in 2015. Having received her PhD for a thesis on Korean feminist poetics, she teaches at Gyeongsang National University. She is also a newspaper columnist and hosts a poetry-themed radio program. In 2012, she held a residency at the Free University of Berlin as part of the Writer-in-Residence Abroad Program of the Arts Council Korea (ARKO) and in 2016 was a Writer-in-Residence at the University of Ljubljana in Slovenia.

Kim Haeng-sook (born in Seoul – 1970) is a Korean poet and professor. Her debut poem appeared in the quarterly *Contemporary Literature* in 1999. In 2000, she was named the recipient of the Daesan Creative Writing Fund. Her poetry collections include *Adolescence* (2003), *The Ability to Part* (2007), and she has also published book of prose including *What Was Literature* (2005), *Traversing Creations and Ruins* (2005). She also received the Solmoe Creative Writing Fund in 2007. Currently she is professor of Korean literature at Kangnam University.

Jake Levine is the author of two chapbooks, *The Threshold of Erasure* and *Vilna Dybbuk*. He translates Kim Kyung-ju and is currently working on a PhD in comparative literature at Seoul National University. He edits Spork Press and writes a bi-monthly column introducing American poetry to Korea at the Korean webzine *Munjang*.

Ji Yoon Lee is a poet and translator whose most recent publication is a book of translation, *Cheer Up, Femme Fatale* (Action Books, 2015). She is the author of Foreigner's *Folly* (Coconut Books, 2014), *Funsize/Bitesize* (Birds of Lace, 2013) and *IMMA* (Radioactive Moat, 2012). She is the winner of the Joanna Cargill prize (2014), and her manuscript was a finalist for the 1913 First Book Prize (2012). She was born in South Korea, and immigrated to the United States as a teen. She received her MFA in Creative Writing from the University of Notre Dame.

Don Mee Choi was born in Seoul and grew up in Seoul and Hong Kong. She now lives in Seattle. She is the author of *The Morning News is Exciting* (Action Books, 2010) and a recipient of a 2011 Whiting Writers Award and the 2012 Lucien Stryk Translation Prize. Her most recent translation titles are *Princess Abandoned* (Tinfish, 2012), *Sorrowtoothpaste Mirrorcream* (Action Books, 2014), and *I'm OK, I'm Pig!* (Bloodaxe Books, 2014). She has a pamphlet of talks forthcoming from Wave Books. In 2014, her *Petite Manifesto* was published by Vagabond Press and in 2015 the collaborative project *Trilingual Renshi*.

Poet and translator **Johannes Göransson** emigrated with his family from Skåne, Sweden to the United States at age 13. He earned a BA from the University of Minnesota, an MFA from the Iowa Writers' Workshop, and his PhD from the University of Georgia. He is the author of several books, including *Haute Surveillance* (2013), *Entrance to a colonial pageant in which we all begin to intricate* (2011), and *Dear Ra (A Story in Flinches)*(2008). He has translated Aase Berg's *Dark Matter* (2012), *Transfer Fat* (2012), and *Remainland: Selected Poems of Aase Berg* (2005) as well as Henry Parland's *Ideals Clearance* (2007).